BAND TECHNIQUE
STEP-BY-STEP
ROBERT ELLEDGE · DONALD HADDAD

Warm-up and Practice Suggestions

Make practicing part of your daily schedule. If you plan it as you do any other activity, you will find plenty of time for it. Find a place to practice that is free of distractions, and try to practice there every day. Use the following *STEP-BY-STEP* procedure as a practicing guide:

1. Begin every practice session or group rehearsal by taking some deep breaths, clearing your mind of distractions.

2. Continue with a regular and familiar warm-up routine including repeated sticking patterns, roll studies, and simple techical exercises. Like an athlete, you need to warm up your mind and muscles before you begin performing.

3. Include time in every practice session for work on your lesson assignment, and any rough spots in your band music. Use of a metronome is helpful. Tape record yourself, and critically evaluate your playing.

4. Spend time sightreading new material and practicing the International Drum Rudiments.

5. Conclude your practice session by playing something fun and enjoyable.

Learning to play a musical instrument is a rewarding and challenging experience. Diligent practice is the key to reaching your musical goals!

*The authors wish to thank **Chuck Elledge** for providing the Percussion Private Lessons found at the end of each unit. An active educator, performer, and composer, Mr. Elledge received his Bachelor of Music degree from the University of Minnesota. He is currently Staff Writer at the Neil A. Kjos Music Company in San Diego, California, and serves as Music Director for the Minnesota Vikings Football Club.*

ISBN 0-8497-8516-2

KJOS NEIL A. KJOS MUSIC COMPANY ■ SAN DIEGO, CALIFORNIA

⌐ UNIT ONE ⌐
CONCERT B♭ MAJOR

1. Intonation Study

LESSON 1

2. Major Scale Study

3. Tonguing Study

LESSON 2

4. Scale Study

5. Rhythm Studies

Basic

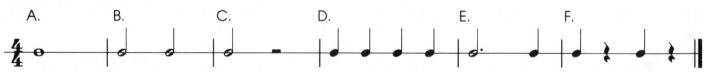

Advanced

LESSON 3

6. Major Chord Study

7. Interval Study

8. Melodic Rhythm Studies

Basic

Advanced

LESSON 4

9. Thirds Study

10. Harmonic Study   TACET

11. Private Lesson

☐ Practice this roll development study on various notes.   ☐ Use alternate sticking throughout (no double strokes).
☐ Practice beginning both with the right and left hand.

⌐ UNIT TWO ⌐
CONCERT G MINOR

12. Intonation Study

LESSON 1

13. Minor Scale Study

14. Tonguing Study

LESSON 2

15. Scale Study

16. Rhythm Studies

Basic

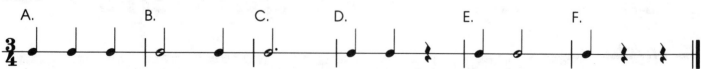

Advanced

LESSON 3

17. Minor Chord Study

18. Interval Study

19. Melodic Rhythm Studies

Basic

Advanced

LESSON 4

20. Thirds Study

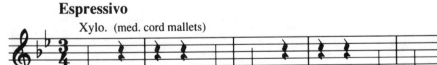

21. Harmonic Study

22. Private Lesson

☐ Start slowly and work for speed and accuracy.

UNIT THREE
CONCERT E♭ MAJOR

23. Intonation Study

LESSON 1

24. Major Scale Study

25. Tonguing Study

LESSON 2

26. Scale Study

27. Rhythm Studies

Basic

Advanced

LESSON 3

28. Major Chord Study

29. Interval Study

30. Melodic Rhythm Studies

Basic

Advanced

LESSON 4

31. Thirds Study

32. Harmonic Study

Cantabile

Bells (med. rubber mallets)

33. Private Lesson

☐ Start slowly and work for speed and accuracy.

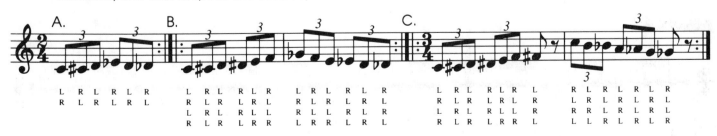

⌐ UNIT FOUR ⌐
CONCERT C MINOR

34. Intonation Study

LESSON 1

35. Minor Scale Study

36. Tonguing Study

LESSON 2

37. Scale Study

38. Rhythm Studies
Basic

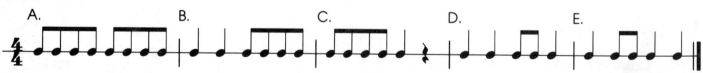

Advanced

LESSON 3

39. Minor Chord Study

40. Interval Study

41. Melodic Rhythm Studies

Basic

Advanced

LESSON 4

42. Thirds Study

43. Harmonic Study   TACET

44. Private Lesson

☐ Try a variety of stickings.   ☐ Start slowly and work for speed and accuracy.

⌐ UNIT FIVE ⌐
CONCERT F MAJOR

45. Intonation Study

LESSON 1

46. Major Scale Study

47. Tonguing Study

LESSON 2

48. Scale Study

49. Rhythm Studies
Basic

Advanced

LESSON 3

50. Major Chord Study

51. Interval Study

52. Melodic Rhythm Studies

Basic

Advanced

LESSON 4

53. Thirds Study

54. Harmonic Study

55. Private Lesson

☐ Try a variety of stickings on these whole tone scale studies.　　☐ Start slowly and work for speed and accuracy.

⌐ UNIT SIX ¬
CONCERT D MINOR

56. Intonation Study

LESSON 1

57. Minor Scale Study

58. Tonguing Study

LESSON 2

59. Scale Study

60. Rhythm Studies

Basic

Advanced

LESSON 3

61. Minor Chord Study

62. Interval Study

63. Melodic Rhythm Studies

Basic

Advanced

LESSON 4

64. Thirds Study

65. Harmonic Study

TACET

66. Private Lesson

☐ Practice these cross sticking studies slowly at first. As much as possible, position your mallets over the appropriate bars before striking them. ☐ Also try using alternate sticking on B. and C.

⌐ UNIT SEVEN ¬
CONCERT A♭ MAJOR

67. Intonation Study

LESSON 1

68. Major Scale Study

69. Tonguing Study

LESSON 2

70. Scale Study

71. Rhythm Studies
Basic

Advanced

LESSON 3

72. Major Chord Study

73. Interval Study

74. Melodic Rhythm Studies

Basic

Advanced

LESSON 4

75. Thirds Study

76. Harmonic Study

77. Private Lesson

☐ At first, practice each exercise at a constant dynamic level without accents.

♫ UNIT EIGHT ♫
CONCERT F MINOR

78. Intonation Study

LESSON 1

79. Minor Scale Study

80. Tonguing Study

LESSON 2

81. Scale Study

82. Rhythm Studies

Basic

Advanced

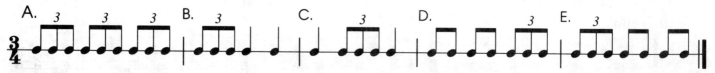

LESSON 3

83. Minor Chord Study

84. Interval Study

85. Melodic Rhythm Studies

Basic

Advanced

LESSON 4

86. Thirds Study

87. Harmonic Study

TACET

88. Private Lesson

☐ Start slowly and work for speed and accuracy.   ☐ Use a metronome to measure your progress.

⌐ UNIT NINE ¬

CONCERT D♭ MAJOR

89. Intonation Study

LESSON 1

90. Major Scale Study

91. Tonguing Study

LESSON 2

92. Scale Study

93. Rhythm Studies

Basic

Advanced

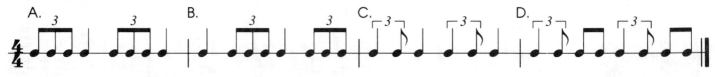

LESSON 3

94. Major Chord Study

95. Interval Study

96. Melodic Rhythm Studies

Basic

Advanced

LESSON 4

97. Thirds Study

98. Harmonic Study   TACET

99. Private Lesson

☐ At first, practice each measure separately.   ☐ After learning this exercise as written, play with all doublestops rolled.
☐ The chord symbol above each measure designates the major chord being played.

⌐ UNIT TEN ⌐

CONCERT B♭ MINOR

100. Intonation Study

LESSON 1

101. Minor Scale Study

102. Tonguing Study

LESSON 2

103. Scale Study

104. Rhythm Studies

Basic

Advanced

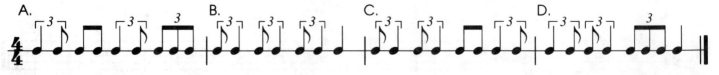

LESSON 3

105. Minor Chord Study

106. Interval Study

107. Melodic Rhythm Studies

Basic

Advanced

LESSON 4

108. Thirds Study

109. Harmonic Study

TACET

110. Private Lesson

☐ At first, practice each measure separately. ☐ After learning this exercise as written, play with all doublestops rolled.
☐ The chord symbol above each measure designates the minor chord being played.

⌐ UNIT ELEVEN ⌐

CONCERT C MAJOR

111. Intonation Study

LESSON 1

112. Major Scale Study

113. Tonguing Study

LESSON 2

114. Scale Study

115. Rhythm Studies

Basic

Advanced

LESSON 3

116. Major Chord Study

117. Interval Study

118. Melodic Rhythm Studies

Basic

mp

Advanced

mf

LESSON 4

119. Thirds Study

120. Harmonic Study

TACET

121. Private Lesson

☐ At first, practice each measure separately.
☐ After learning this exercise as written, play with all notes and doublestops rolled.
☐ The chord symbol above each measure designates the dominant seventh chord being played.

⌐ UNIT TWELVE ⌐
CONCERT A MINOR

122. Intonation Study

LESSON 1

123. Minor Scale Study

124. Tonguing Study

LESSON 2

125. Scale Study

126. Rhythm Studies

Basic

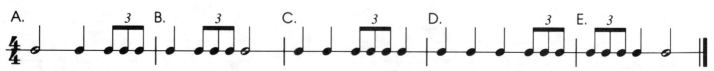

Advanced

LESSON 3

127. Minor Chord Study

128. Interval Study

129. Melodic Rhythm Studies

Basic

Advanced

LESSON 4

130. Thirds Study

131. Harmonic Study

Freely

Bells (med. rubber mallets)

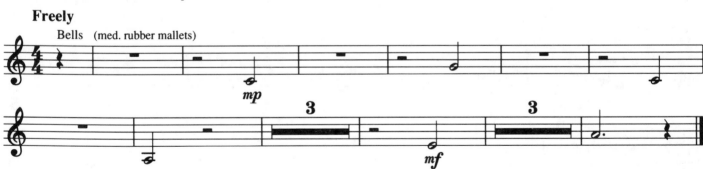

132. Private Lesson

☐ For additional practice, repeat each triplet two, three, or four times. ☐ Also try using alternate sticking.
☐ The chord symbols designate the major chord being played.

C	C#	D	Eb	E	F	F#	G	Ab	A	Bb	B	C

⌐ UNIT THIRTEEN ⌐

CONCERT G MAJOR

133. Intonation Study

LESSON 1

134. Major Scale Study

135. Tonguing Study

LESSON 2

136. Scale Study

137. Rhythm Studies

Basic

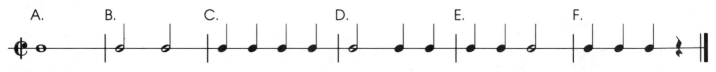

Advanced

LESSON 3

138. Major Chord Study

139. Interval Study

140. Melodic Rhythm Studies

Basic

Advanced

LESSON 4

141. Thirds Study

142. Harmonic Study

143. Private Lesson

☐ For additional practice, repeat each triplet two, three, or four times. ☐ Also try using alternate sticking.
☐ The chord symbols designate the major chord being played.

⌐ UNIT FOURTEEN ⌐
CONCERT E MINOR

144. Intonation Study

LESSON 1

145. Minor Scale Study

146. Tonguing Study

LESSON 2

147. Scale Study

148. Rhythm Studies
Basic

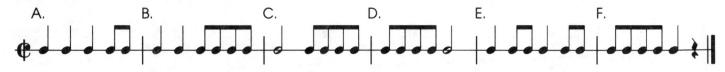

Advanced

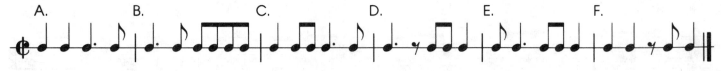

LESSON 3

149. Minor Chord Study

150. Interval Study

151. Melodic Rhythm Studies

Basic

Advanced

LESSON 4

152. Thirds Study

153. Harmonic Study   TACET

154. Private Lesson

☐ Practice this theme from Haydn's *"Surprise" Symphony* slowly and carefully; strive for accuracy.
☐ On glissandos, slide the mallet over the natural bars only, striking the primary note with a mallet in the other hand.
☐ On trills (*tr〰*), rapidly alternate between the indicated note and the next highest note in the key.

⌐ UNIT FIFTEEN ⌐

CONCERT D MAJOR

155. Intonation Study

LESSON 1

156. Major Scale Study

157. Tonguing Study

LESSON 2

158. Scale Study

159. Rhythm Studies

Basic

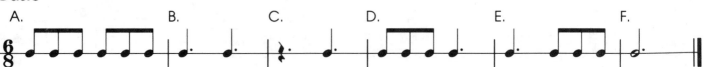

Advanced

LESSON 3

160. Major Chord Study

161. Interval Study

162. Melodic Rhythm Studies

Basic

Advanced

LESSON 4

163. Thirds Study

164. Harmonic Study

Adagietto

165. Private Lesson

☐ Holding two mallets in each hand, play this exercise three ways: 1) right hand only 2) left hand only 3) alternating hands.
☐ For additional study, play exercises #88, #99, #110, and #121 in the same three ways.

⌐ UNIT SIXTEEN ⌐

CONCERT B MINOR

166. Intonation Study

LESSON 1

167. Minor Scale Study

168. Tonguing Study

LESSON 2

169. Scale Study

170. Rhythm Studies
Basic

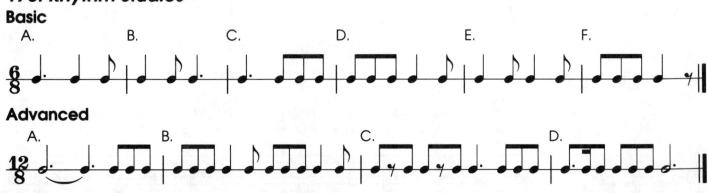

Advanced

LESSON 3

171. Minor Chord Study

172. Interval Study

173. Melodic Rhythm Studies

Basic

Advanced

sempre f

LESSON 4

174. Thirds Study

175. Harmonic Study

TACET

176. Private Lesson

☐ Roll some or all of the chords after learning this exercise as written.
☐ The chord symbols designate the major and dominant seventh chords being played.

⌐⌐ CONCERT CHORALES ⌐⌐

I. Espressivo

TACET

II. Andantino

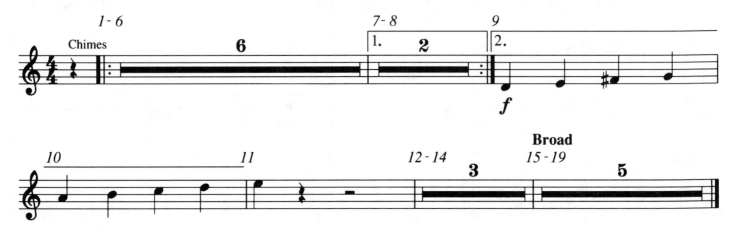

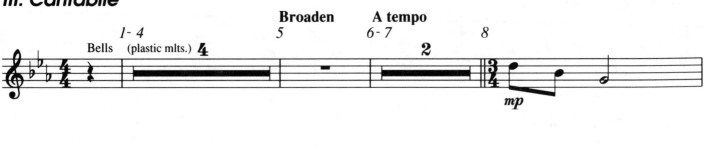

III. Cantabile

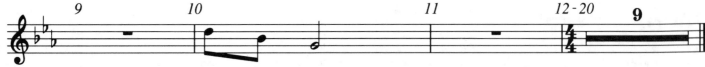

IV. Rubato

⌐ STEP-BY-STEP PROGRESS CHART ⌐

	Intonation	LESSON 1			LESSON 2			LESSON 3			LESSON 4		Private Lesson
		Major/Scale Minor	Tonguing	Scale	Rhythm		Major/Chord Minor	Interval	Melodic Rhythm		Thirds	Harmonic	
					Basic	Advanced			Basic	Advanced			
UNIT 1													
UNIT 2													
UNIT 3													
UNIT 4													
UNIT 5													
UNIT 6													
UNIT 7													
UNIT 8													
UNIT 9													
UNIT 10													
UNIT 11													
UNIT 12													
UNIT 13													
UNIT 14													
UNIT 15													
UNIT 16													

⌐ UNIT ONE ⌐

CONCERT B♭ MAJOR

1. Intonation Study   TACET

LESSON 1

2. Major Scale Study (Accent and Flam Study)

3. Tonguing Study (Double Stroke Study)

LESSON 2

4. Scale Study (Sticking Study)

5. Rhythm Studies

Basic

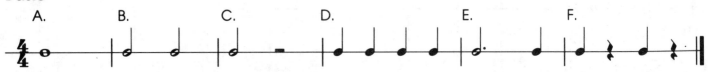

Advanced

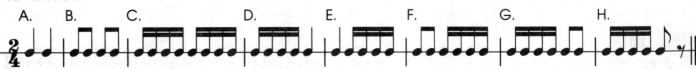

LESSON 3

6. Major Chord Study (Flam Study)

7. Interval Study (Drag Study)

8. Melodic Rhythm Studies

Basic

Advanced

LESSON 4

9. Thirds Study (Roll Study)

10. Harmonic Study

11. Private Lesson

☐ In exercise E., repeat each measure separately or play as written.

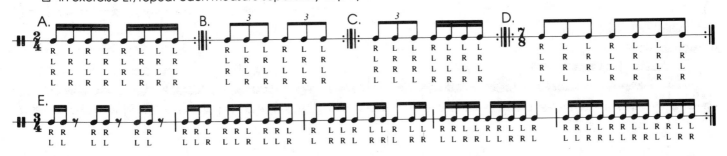

⌐ UNIT TWO ⌐
CONCERT G MINOR

12. Intonation Study   TACET

LESSON 1

13. Minor Scale Study (Accent and Flam Study)

14. Tonguing Study (Double Stroke Study)

LESSON 2

15. Scale Study (Sticking Study)

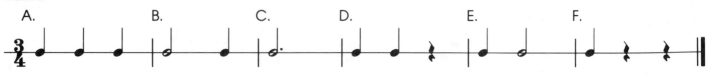

16. Rhythm Studies

Basic

Advanced

LESSON 3

17. Minor Chord Study (Flam Study)

18. Interval Study (Drag Study)

19. Melodic Rhythm Studies

Basic

Advanced

LESSON 4

20. Thirds Study (Roll Study)

21. Harmonic Study   TACET

22. Private Lesson

To play a multiple bounce stroke (indicated by "z" through the stem):

☐ Allow the stick to bounce freely (usually five or more times) following the initial stroke.
☐ Complete the stroke with an upstroke *before* the stick stops bouncing.

ᒯ UNIT THREE ᒪ
CONCERT Eᵇ MAJOR

23. Intonation Study   TACET

LESSON 1

24. Major Scale Study (Accent and Flam Study)

25. Tonguing Study (Double Stroke Study)

LESSON 2

26. Scale Study (Sticking Study)

27. Rhythm Studies

Basic

Advanced

LESSON 3

28. Major Chord Study (Flam Study)

29. Interval Study (Drag Study)

30. Melodic Rhythm Studies

Basic

Advanced

LESSON 4

31. Thirds Study (Roll Study)

32. Harmonic Study　　　　TACET

33. Private Lesson

- ☐ The multiple bounce roll is also known as the buzz roll, closed roll, concert roll, and orchestral roll.
- ☐ In each study, play each measure the same, using multiple bounce strokes to create the rolls.
- ☐ Strive for a smooth, even sound when playing multiple bounce rolls.

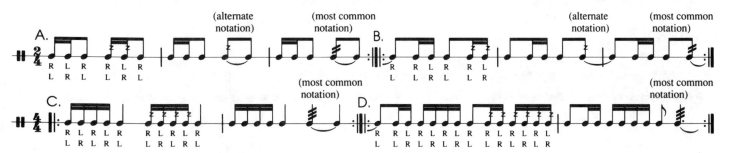

⌐ UNIT FOUR ⌐
CONCERT C MINOR

34. Intonation Study
TACET

LESSON 1

35. Minor Scale Study (Accent and Flam Study)

36. Tonguing Study (Double Stroke Study)

LESSON 2

37. Scale Study (Sticking Study)

38. Rhythm Studies

Basic

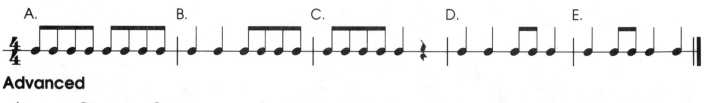

Advanced

LESSON 3

39. Minor Chord Study (Flam Study)

40. Interval Study (Drag Study)

41. Melodic Rhythm Studies

Basic

Advanced

LESSON 4

42. Thirds Study (Roll Study)

43. Harmonic Study

44. Private Lesson

☐ In each study, play each measure the same, using multiple bounce strokes to create the rolls.
☐ Strive for a smooth, even sound when playing multiple bounce rolls.

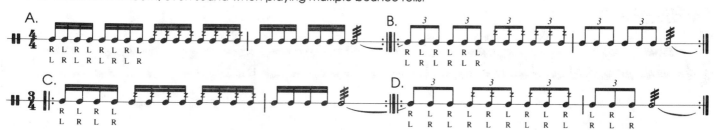

⌐ UNIT FIVE ⌐
CONCERT F MAJOR

45. Intonation Study

TACET

LESSON 1

46. Major Scale Study (Accent and Flam Study)

47. Tonguing Study (Double Stroke Study)

LESSON 2

48. Scale Study (Sticking Study)

49. Rhythm Studies

Basic

Advanced

LESSON 3

50. *Major Chord Study (Flam Study)*

51. *Interval Study (Drag Study)*

52. *Melodic Rhythm Studies*

Basic

Advanced

LESSON 4

53. *Thirds Study (Roll Study)*

54. *Harmonic Study*   TACET

55. *Private Lesson*

□ Strive for a smooth, even sound when playing multiple bounce rolls.

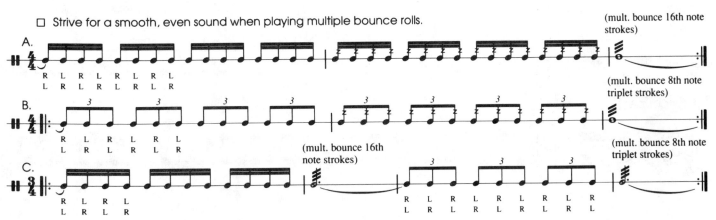

⌐ UNIT SIX ⌐
CONCERT D MINOR

56. Intonation Study

TACET

LESSON 1

57. Minor Scale Study (Accent and Flam Study)

58. Tonguing Study (Double Stroke Study)

LESSON 2

59. Scale Study (Sticking Study)

60. Rhythm Studies

Basic

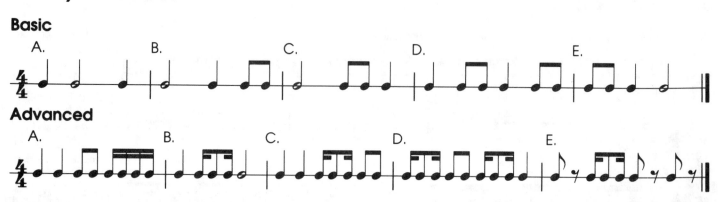

Advanced

LESSON 3

61. Minor Chord Study (Flam Study)

62. Interval Study (Drag Study)

63. Melodic Rhythm Studies

Basic

Advanced

LESSON 4

64. Thirds Study (Roll Study)

65. Harmonic Study

Espressivo

Sus. Cym. (yarn mlts.)

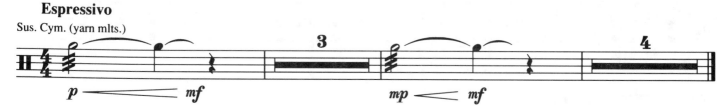

66. Private Lesson

☐ After mastering the exercise at a constant **mf**, play using the given dynamics.   ☐ Work for speed.

⌐ UNIT SEVEN ⌐
CONCERT A♭ MAJOR

67. Intonation Study   TACET

LESSON 1

68. Major Scale Study (Accent and Flam Study)

69. Tonguing Study (Double Stroke Study)

LESSON 2

70. Scale Study (Sticking Study)

71. Rhythm Studies

Basic

Advanced

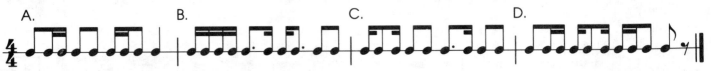

LESSON 3

72. Major Chord Study (Flam Study)

73. Interval Study (Drag Study)

74. Melodic Rhythm Studies

Basic

Advanced

LESSON 4

75. Thirds Study (Roll Study)

76. Harmonic Study

TACET

77. Private Lesson

☐ After mastering the exercises at a constant *mf*, play using the given dynamics.

⌐ UNIT EIGHT ¬
CONCERT F MINOR

78. Intonation Study   TACET

LESSON 1

79. Minor Scale Study (Accent and Flam Study)

80. Tonguing Study (Double Stroke Study)

LESSON 2

81. Scale Study (Sticking Study)

82. Rhythm Studies

Basic

Advanced

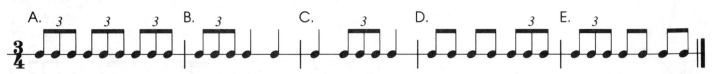

LESSON 3

83. Minor Chord Study (Flam Study)

84. Interval Study (Drag Study)

85. Melodic Rhythm Studies

Basic

Advanced

LESSON 4

86. Thirds Study (Roll Study)

87. Harmonic Study

Cantabile

Sus. Cym.
(yarn mlts.)

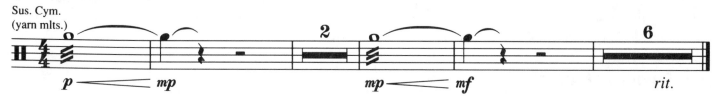

88. Private Lesson

☐ Practice each pattern two ways: 1) right hand on cymbal or snare drum rim, left hand on snare 2) left hand on cymbal or snare drum rim, right hand on snare.

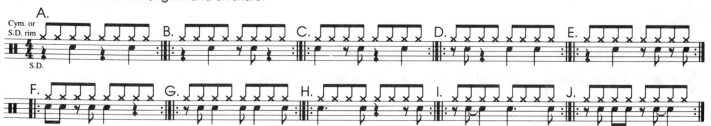

⌐ UNIT NINE ¬
CONCERT D♭ MAJOR

89. Intonation Study   TACET

LESSON 1

90. Major Scale Study (Accent and Flam Study)

91. Tonguing Study (Double Stroke Study)

LESSON 2

92. Scale Study (Sticking Study)

93. Rhythm Studies

Basic

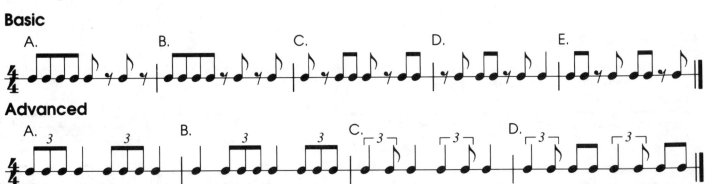

Advanced

LESSON 3

94. Major Chord Study (Flam Study)

95. Interval Study (Drag Study)

96. Melodic Rhythm Studies

Basic

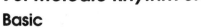

Advanced

LESSON 4

97. Thirds Study (Roll Study)

98. Harmonic Study

99. Private Lesson

☐ Practice each pattern two ways: 1) right hand on cymbal or snare drum rim, left hand on snare 2) left hand on cymbal or snare drum rim, right hand on snare.

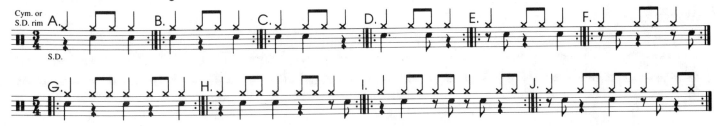

⌐ UNIT TEN ¬
CONCERT B♭ MINOR

100. Intonation Study   TACET

LESSON 1

101. Minor Scale Study (Accent and Flam Study)

102. Tonguing Study (Double Stroke Study)

LESSON 2

103. Scale Study (Sticking Study)

104. Rhythm Studies
Basic

Advanced

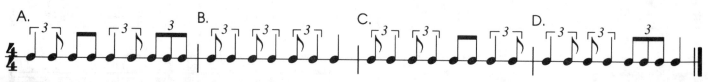

LESSON 3

105. Minor Chord Study (Flam Study)

106. Interval Study (Drag Study)

107. Melodic Rhythm Studies

Basic

Advanced

LESSON 4

108. Thirds Study (Roll Study)

109. Harmonic Study

110. Private Lesson

☐ Practice each pattern two ways: 1) right hand on cymbal or snare drum rim, left hand on snare 2) left hand on cymbal or snare drum rim, right hand on snare.

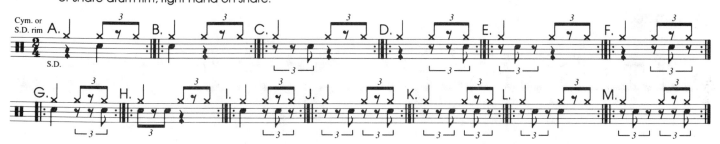

⌐ UNIT ELEVEN ⌐
CONCERT C MAJOR

111. Intonation Study   TACET

LESSON 1

112. Major Scale Study (Accent and Flam Study)

113. Tonguing Study (Double Stroke Study)

LESSON 2

114. Scale Study (Sticking Study)

115. Rhythm Studies

Basic

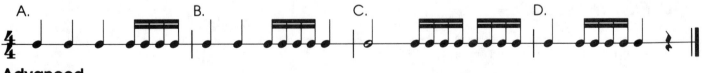

Advanced

LESSON 3

116. Major Chord Study (Flam Study)

117. Interval Study (Drag Study)

118. Melodic Rhythm Studies

Basic

Advanced

LESSON 4

119. Thirds Study (Roll Study)

120. Harmonic Study

121. Private Lesson

☐ Practice each pattern three ways: 1) with accents only 2) with dynamics only 3) with both accents and dynamics.
☐ Practice patterns C. and D. using various stickings.

⌐ UNIT TWELVE ¬
CONCERT A MINOR

122. Intonation Study

TACET

LESSON 1

123. Minor Scale Study (Accent and Flam Study)

124. Tonguing Study (Double Stroke Study)

LESSON 2

125. Scale Study (Sticking Study)

126. Rhythm Studies

Basic

Advanced

LESSON 3

127. Minor Chord Study (Flam Study)

128. Interval Study (Drag Study)

129. Melodic Rhythm Studies

Basic

Advanced

LESSON 4

130. Thirds Study (Roll Study)

131. Harmonic Study   TACET

132. Private Lesson

☐ Use this study to develop your ability to accelerate and decelerate gradually when playing double stroke open rolls.

⌐ UNIT THIRTEEN ⌐
CONCERT G MAJOR

133. Intonation Study   TACET

LESSON 1

134. Major Scale Study (Accent and Flam Study)

135. Tonguing Study (Double Stroke Study)

LESSON 2

136. Scale Study (Sticking Study)

137. Rhythm Studies

Basic

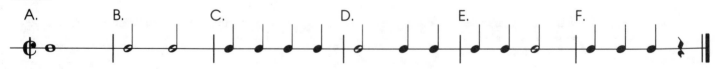

Advanced

LESSON 3

138. Major Chord Study (Flam Study)

139. Interval Study (Drag Study)

140. Melodic Rhythm Studies

Basic

Advanced

LESSON 4

141. Thirds Study (Roll Study)

142. Harmonic Study   TACET

143. Private Lesson

- ☐ Practice these mixed meter patterns with and without accents, and at a variety of dynamic levels.
- ☐ Try various stickings. ☐ Repeat each pattern separately *and* play as one continuous study.
- ☐ For additional practice, play two sixteenth notes in place of any eighth note *ad lib.*

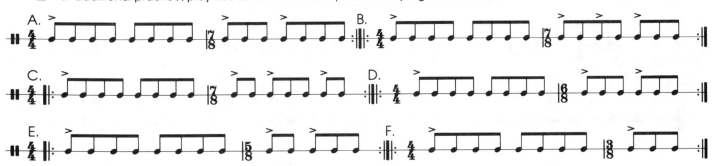

⌐ UNIT FOURTEEN ⌐
CONCERT E MINOR

144. Intonation Study   TACET

LESSON 1

145. Minor Scale Study (Accent and Flam Study)

146. Tonguing Study (Double Stroke Study)

LESSON 2

147. Scale Study (Sticking Study)

148. Rhythm Studies

Basic

Advanced

LESSON 3

149. Minor Chord Study (Flam Study)

150. Interval Study (Drag Study)

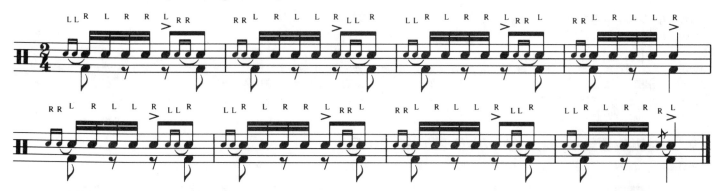

151. Melodic Rhythm Studies

Basic

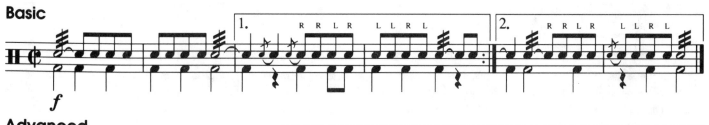

Advanced

LESSON 4

152. Thirds Study (Roll Study)

153. Harmonic Study   TACET

154. Private Lesson

☐ Practice these mixed meter patterns with and without accents, and at a variety of dynamic levels.
☐ Try various stickings.   ☐ Repeat each pattern separately *and* play as one continuous study.
☐ For additional practice, play two sixteenth notes in place of any eighth note *ad lib.*

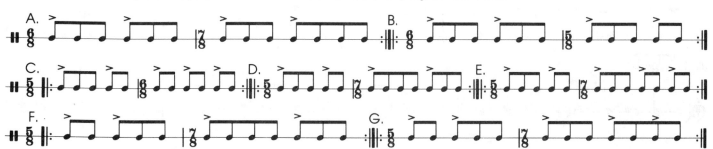

UNIT FIFTEEN
CONCERT D MAJOR

155. Intonation Study
TACET

LESSON 1

156. Major Scale Study (Accent and Flam Study)

157. Tonguing Study (Double Stroke Study)

LESSON 2

158. Scale Study (Sticking Study)

159. Rhythm Studies
Basic

Advanced

LESSON 3

160. Major Chord Study (Flam Study)

161. Interval Study (Drag Study)

162. Melodic Rhythm Studies

Basic

mf

Advanced

f

LESSON 4

163. Thirds Study (Roll Study)

164. Harmonic Study   TACET

165. Private Lesson

☐ Practice these grace note studies at a variety of dynamic levels.   ☐ Play grace notes quickly. The speed of the grace notes should remain the same regardless of the music's tempo.

A.

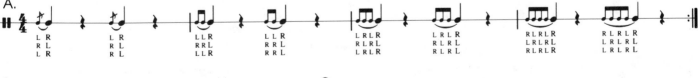

B.   C.

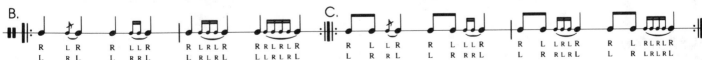

D.

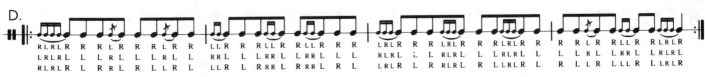

⌐┌ UNIT SIXTEEN ┐┐
CONCERT B MINOR

166. Intonation Study   TACET

LESSON 1

167. Minor Scale Study (Accent and Flam Study)

168. Tonguing Study (Double Stroke Study)

LESSON 2

169. Scale Study (Sticking Study)

170. Rhythm Studies

Basic

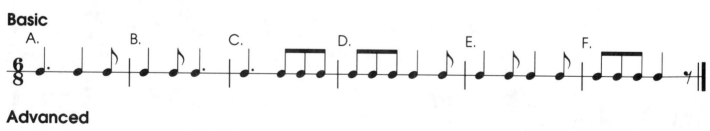

Advanced

LESSON 3

171. Minor Chord Study (Flam Study)

172. Interval Study (Drag Study)

173. Melodic Rhythm Studies

Basic

Advanced

sempre **f**

LESSON 4

174. Thirds Study (Roll Study)

175. Harmonic Study

Grazioso

176. Private Lesson

☐ On this triple stroke roll study, repeat each measure separately or play as written.

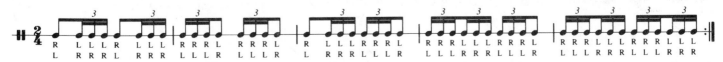

♪ CONCERT CHORALES ♫

I. Espressivo

II. Andantino

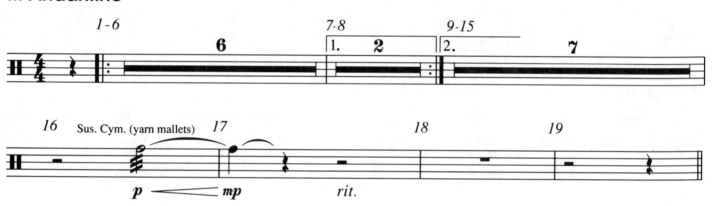

III. Cantabile

TACET

IV. Rubato

TACET

⌐ STEP-BY-STEP PROGRESS CHART ⌐

	Intonation	LESSON 1			LESSON 2			LESSON 3			LESSON 4		
		Major/ Minor Scale	Tonguing	Scale	Rhythm Basic	Advanced	Major/ Chord Minor	Interval	Melodic Rhythm Basic	Advanced	Thirds	Harmonic	Private Lesson
UNIT 1													
UNIT 2													
UNIT 3													
UNIT 4													
UNIT 5													
UNIT 6													
UNIT 7													
UNIT 8													
UNIT 9													
UNIT 10													
UNIT 11													
UNIT 12													
UNIT 13													
UNIT 14													
UNIT 15													
UNIT 16													

PERCUSSIVE ARTS SOCIETY INTERNATIONAL DRUM RUDIMENTS

All rudiments should be practiced: *open* (slow) to *close* (fast) to *open* (slow) and/or at an even moderate march tempo.

I. ROLL RUDIMENTS

A. SINGLE STROKE ROLL RUDIMENTS

1. SINGLE STROKE ROLL *

R L R L R L R L

2. SINGLE STROKE FOUR

R L R L   R L R L
L R L R   L R L R

3. SINGLE STROKE SEVEN

R L R L R L R
L R L R L R L

B. MULTIPLE BOUNCE ROLL RUDIMENTS

4. MULTIPLE BOUNCE ROLL

5. TRIPLE STROKE ROLL

R R R L L L R R R L L L

C. DOUBLE STROKE OPEN ROLL RUDIMENTS

6. DOUBLE STROKE OPEN ROLL *

R R L L R R L L

7. FIVE STROKE ROLL *

R R L L

8. SIX STROKE ROLL
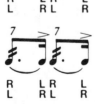
R   L R   L
L   R L   R

9. SEVEN STROKE ROLL *
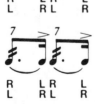
R   L R   L
L   R L   R

10. NINE STROKE ROLL *

R   R   L   L

11. TEN STROKE ROLL *

R   R L   R   R L
L   L R   L   L R

12. ELEVEN STROKE ROLL *
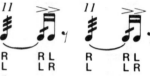
R   R L   R   R L
L   L R   L   L R

13. THIRTEEN STROKE ROLL *

R   R   L   L

14. FIFTEEN STROKE ROLL *
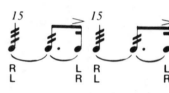
R   L R   L
L   R L   R

15. SEVENTEEN STROKE ROLL

R   R   L   L

II. DIDDLE RUDIMENTS

16. SINGLE PARADIDDLE *

R L R R L R L L

17. DOUBLE PARADIDDLE *

R L R L R R L R L R L L

18. TRIPLE PARADIDDLE

R L R L R L R R L R L R L R L L

19. SINGLE PARADIDDLE-DIDDLE

R L R R L L R L R R L L
L R L L R R L R L L R R

Reprinted with permission of the Percussive Arts Society, Inc.

III. FLAM RUDIMENTS

20. FLAM *

21. FLAM ACCENT *

22. FLAM TAP *

23. FLAMACUE *

24. FLAM PARADIDDLE *

25. SINGLE FLAMMED MILL

26. FLAM PARADIDDLE-DIDDLE *

27. PATAFLAFLA

28. SWISS ARMY TRIPLET

29. INVERTED FLAM TAP

30. FLAM DRAG

IV. DRAG RUDIMENTS

31. DRAG *

32. SINGLE DRAG TAP *

33. DOUBLE DRAG TAP *

34. LESSON 25 *

35. SINGLE DRAGADIDDLE

36. DRAG PARADIDDLE #1*

37. DRAG PARADIDDLE #2 *

38. SINGLE RATAMACUE *

39. DOUBLE RATAMACUE *

40. TRIPLE RATAMACUE *

♪ ADVANCED RHYTHMS ♪

♪ CHROMATIC STUDY ♪